T0368474

AuthorHouse™
1663 Liberty Drive
Bloomington, IN 47403
www.authorhouse.com
Phone: 1 (800) 839-8640

Published by AuthorHouse 06/17/2015

ISBN: 978-1-5049-1786-5 (sc)
ISBN: 978-1-5049-1787-2 (e)

Library of Congress Control Number 2015909600


Print information available on the last page.

authorHOUSE®

# Jump In

## As the Journey Continues

Patty Nelson, Author
Carolyn Smith, Illustrator

# TABLE OF CONTENTS

Special Projects

# Welcome to Mrs. Nelson's Classroom

"Great fun and teaching ideas for Primary grades K-1-2"

# Jump In the Wagon

For kids who want to learn more,
"Jump In the Wagon" for sure!
This book was created
for your teacher and you!
So PEEK inside and take a LOOK!
We think your teacher
will love this BOOK!

BROWN PAPER PACKAGES
TIED UP WITH STRING...
THESE
ARE A FEW
OF
MY FAVORITE THINGS...

# Holiday Art Projects

FIRST CHANCE

SECOND CHANCE

Give students a second chance.

# Classroom Gift for October

Carved by a father of one of my students.

# Mr. Turkey Visits Our Classroom

WOW! THAT'S A BIG TURKEY!

One school year in November, a parent came to me with a fun idea. She told me that since we were creating turkeys for an art project and she had a friend that had a turkey for a pet, she wondered if my students might enjoy having a turkey visit our classroom. Of course, I thought that would be a great experience for everyone. And, it truly was for the children and me!

As you can see in this photo, Mr. Turkey was "up" for this very exciting event!

MR. TURKEY SEEMS TO BE REAL TAME TOO!

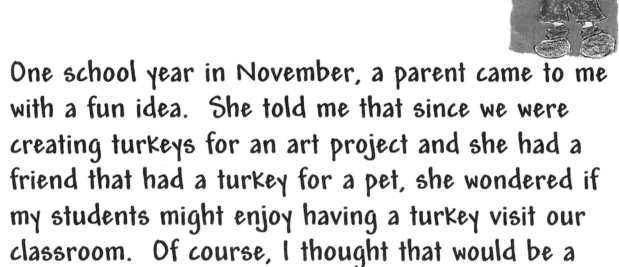

# Handprint Turkey

Created and given to me by one of my proud students!

# Fun Photos

Mr. Turkey visits
us at recess!

Girls only lunch with
Mrs. Nelson!

8

I WAS JOSEPH IN OUR CHRISTMAS CLASS PLAY...

# Kindergarten Christmas Program

This Christmas program was presented to the entire student body at our school, the Kindergarten parents, and the entire community.

While the Kindergarten students acted out the performance, a parent volunteer sang the words for the entire program. Afterward, a holiday party was given for the students and their parents. The Kindergarteners were dismissed after the party to go home with their parents. It was a beautiful way to start the Christmas holiday season.

# Ideas for the Holidays

Holiday sacks for the
"Angels" gifts

Tree Decorations

# Holiday Gifts for Parents

These photos show two samples of holiday gifts made for the students' parents. They were partly prepared in advance by parent volunteers without the parents knowing what the projects would end up being or how they would look.

The angel cans were spray-painted by the parent volunteers and shaped before the students created the face and cheeks on the angel. The students painted pink faces on the cans, which had to dry before they created the facial features. Then, the students drew eyelashes using a black felt-tip marker and added a small black dot for the nose. The wings were made of gold holiday paper attached on the back of the angel with glue. The halo was made from a gold pipe cleaner, formed and glued on the back by each student.

I LOVE ANGELS!

Red felt was donated and cut into bow ties by a parent volunteer who also glued them on the angels.

These holiday angels were packaged (rather than wrapped) in a small white lunch-size paper bag that each student decorated prior to wrapping.

These cute angels proved to be a big hit with the parents, as they were fun, decorative presents created by their children for the holidays.

Another fun holiday gift that my students who celebrate Christmas made for their parents was a button-decorated wooden Christmas tree. The wood was supplied by a local merchant and cut out by a parent volunteer. The buttons were glued on the tree with a parent volunteer using a glue gun.
(This is a good way to get fathers involved in their children's classes!)

I THINK MY DAD CAN CUT THE TREES FOR OUR CLASS! I'M GOING TO ASK HIM...

The students painted their trees and brought in old buttons they had at home. The buttons were collected and each student chose about a dozen different buttons to add to his or her tree. A parent volunteer came into the classroom to help monitor the painting of the trees. The students added white snowflakes, buttons, and bows with the help of a volunteer. All involved had fun, and it was a wonderful memory for those students whose families celebrate Christmas. (See photo of tree on next page.)

Students who do not celebrate Christmas can make snowflakes using white or light blue construction paper and sprinkle glitter on it after cutting. Add white or blue yarn for hanging purposes.

Another possibility is to make snowflakes from Popsicle sticks glued together (with the help of a parent volunteer) with a glue gun. Sprinkle the sticks with glitter and add a piece of yarn for hanging in the windows or on a doorknob.

# A Fun January Snowman Art Project

During the month of January, purchase three Styrofoam balls, diminished in size, to build a snowman. These foam balls can be purchased at Michael's crafts stores.

When stacked upon each other, the height of our snowman was approximately twenty inches. Have a parent place a wood dowel through the middle of the three Styrofoam balls to create the snowman's shape. The snow, on the body of Mr. Snowman, is made of facial-tissue flowers (using pipe cleaners to hold each flower together) made by the students with the help of parent volunteers.

Snowman Poem

Mr. Snowman, round and fat,
All dressed up with a black cravat.
Sticks for arms and buttons for eyes,
My, you look so proud and wise!

Ask for volunteer parents (who want to help and can only do so at home) to start making tissue flowers by using a pipe cleaner placed in the center of each folded tissue flower, twisted to hold the flower together. Then, have students fan the folded blooming part of the flower by spreading the tissue layers apart.

Have a volunteer mother help in the class room to place and secure the "snow flowers" on the snowman's body. Use a screwdriver to make a small hole in the body of the snowman in which to place the pipe cleaner flower wires of the bloom. Add a small amount of glue on the tip of each of the pipe cleaners to secure them in the body.

After all of the snow flowers are in position on the snowman's body, add the twig arms, button eyes and the buttons on the front of the snowman's body. Next, add a carrot nose, cravat, (a neckerchief, which is probably a new vocabulary word for your students) and top with a stocking cap. Place Mr. Snowman on a table where the students can sit around him and enjoy their January art project while they read.

Find some fun songs to sing about snowmen or ask the music teacher to teach your students some snowman songs. Also, read a few snowman stories to your students. This is a fun, unique, and creative activity to do during the month of January.

We even used our snowman project for a math estimation lesson. The parents counted the Kleenex flowers when placing them on the snowman body.

Each student wrote their estimated number on a piece of paper with his or her name and put it in the estimation can. This was a fun way to introduce another new math concept. Another activity we did using the snowman was to have a parent volunteer take a photo of each student with our cute class snowman. I placed this photo on a paper labeled "January Fun Art Project" and it was placed in each student's end-of-the-school-year scrapbook.

Enjoy creating this fun and great activity during the month of January to stimulate your students when they come back to school after the holiday season. It is a unique and fun way to start off the new year at school!

# Mother's Day Gift
## Art Project

Using green construction paper (9" x 12"), fold in half horizontally, then draw a line 1½" up from the bottom edges, which is a stopping point for cutting.  Next, students cut lines, <u>starting at the fold</u>, which have been drawn ¾" apart from the fold to the line that is 1½" from the bottom edge.  Have students stop cutting at the 1½" line that has already been drawn on the folded green paper. (See illustration and photo)

When cutting has been completed, <u>turn the cut piece inside out</u> and wind the base in a circle. This makes the stems for the bouquet. Staple it at the base to hold the circular shape.  Have students draw flower blossoms on white paper, color, and cut out.  Glue blossoms on the fold of each stem until all stem folds have a blossom.

Add colored tissue paper at the base of the flowers and tie a bow with yarn or ribbon about two inches up from the base.  Or, if possible, place the bouquet in a small terra cotta pot, as pictured below, but you remember that you will still need to staple the base. Have your students make a gift card (use 3" x 5" file card) and secure it on a plastic
stem holder that can be purchased or donated from a florist. (See photos on following page.)

This Mother's Day Gift was a big hit with the moms. The daughter of the secretary at our district office was in my class. When I was at the district office, I saw the bouquet on her desk.  She commented that she had gotten many compliments on her bouquet---a fun and easy Mother's Day gift.

# Mother's Day Bouquet

## Step 1

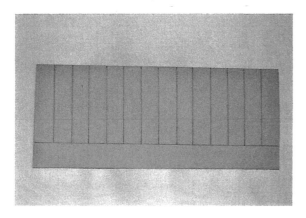

## Step 2

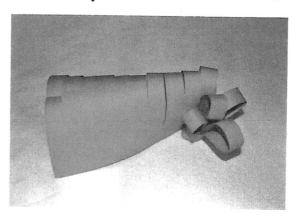

## Step 3

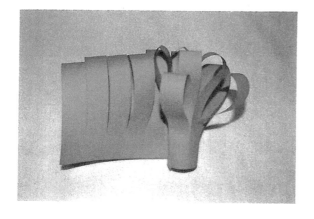

## Step 4

## Step 5

## Step 6

# Bunny Art Container

Have a parent volunteer spray paint
small size cans silver and add a wire handle.
Students add paper ears and make facial
features using a permanent black marker.
Glue a cotton ball in the back for a tail.
Stuff the container with grass and candy.

# Kindergarten Spanish Class Challenges Jr. High Spanish Class

During the school year, a parent at our school was working with some of the junior high students who wanted to learn Spanish. My kindergarten class wanted to learn Spanish also, since several of our kindergarteners were Spanish-speaking only. So, the parent and I set up the same vocabulary for the junior high students and the kindergarteners to study for a period of six weeks.

At the end of this six weeks' study of Spanish in the junior high class and our kindergarten classroom, much fun and learning was accomplished. So, the challenge date was set! I think the junior high students were more nervous than my kindergarten students. It was a very close challenge! The junior high students won by one point. It was a fun and new adventure for all the students. Afterwards both kindergarteners and junior high students went to the Kindergarten playground and had a fun playtime together after some refreshments were served.

What a fun, special way to connect our older students to the younger students at our school. Everyone who attended had a great time.

And, to make a final note, it was the opinion of the adults present that the junior high students were way more nervous than the kindergarten students! What a very fun and memorable time for all involved!

# "Spanish Challenge" Photos of the Adults

Parent/Spanish Teacher for Kindergarteners

Superintendent, School Principal, K-Teacher

# Mother Goose Unit
## Bulletin Board, Art Ideas, Performance & Party

mother goose

Once upon a time

mg

Mother Goose
Mother Goose
MOTHER GOOSE
Mother Goose

# Count your students as blessings.

Education is not filling a pail but the lighting of a fire.
William Yeats

# Welcome to
# Mother Goose Land

# It's Mother Goose Time

After having a fun unit on Mother Goose rhymes, our class had a Mother Goose play for the parents and a party afterward. This took place in October (in the classroom) instead of a Halloween party. It was such a fun way to start the school year after being in class for approximately two and a half months.

The students were familiar with the Mother Goose rhymes, so having a play for the parents at the end of the unit was very rewarding to them. It also gave the parents an opportunity to see their children with their classmates after being in school for just a short period of time. Meeting the parents of their children's classmates was also very beneficial to parents.

The students were dressed in the play as their appointed Mother Goose character. The parents helped create their child's costume with a little help, if needed, from the teacher.

The parents, as you can imagine, loved seeing their children performing the rhymes and having speaking arts.  (We used a microphone, which was also a big hit with the children!) It also gave the parents an opportunity to see the class, meet their child's classmates' parents, and have fun watching the students perform.  It is a great way to start a school year with this age group.

A party was also held after the play in our classroom instead of a Halloween party. A mother of one of the students played the part of Mother Goose during the play and afterward at the classroom party. Mother Goose passed out candy treats from her "many pocket apron."

The parents stayed for the party, and after the party, the students were dismissed.

The room mother coordinated the party. Volunteer mothers made and decorated goose cookies. They served "peas porridge hot, cold, and nine days old," punch, and "three blind mice" cookies. (Recipes for peas porridge and three blind mice cookies are on the following pages).

The party was held in our classroom. A wonderful time was had by all in attendance.

This is a GREAT WAY to start off the school year with the kindergarteners and their parents.

# The Old Woman in the Shoe's Home

After students memorized and individually recited a nursery rhyme they were given a happy face sticker to put on their "Old Woman's Shoe."

*Shoe designed
by
Roberta Clark

Reproducible page for "Mother Goose Rhymes" memorization stickers.

# Mother Goose Photo Fun

Mother Goose Classroom Bulletin Board

A Mother Goose hanging made by a
student's mother

# Mother Goose
# Party Apron
## Covered with Pockets and Filled with Treats

# Mother Goose Land

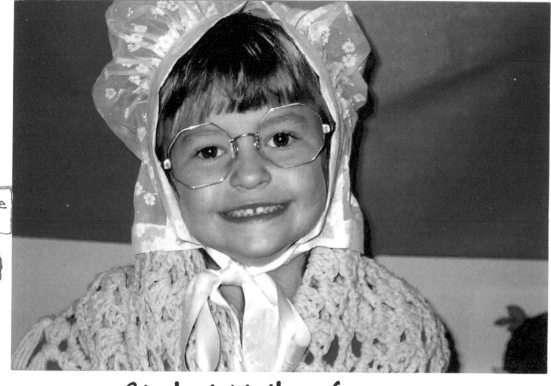

Student Mother Goose
Parent Mother Goose

# Mother Goose Props

I LIKE THE PROPS FOR OUR MOTHER GOOSE PLAY!

Haystack for
Little Boy Blue

Old MacDonald's
Farm

The Old Woman
in the Shoe

I LOVE KINDERGARTEN!

# Mother Goose Performance

## Play held in the classroom

# Mother Goose Quiz

After our Mother Goose play and before our classroom party started, my students and I wrote questions for the parents to answer. A couple of examples of the questions we made up for them are:

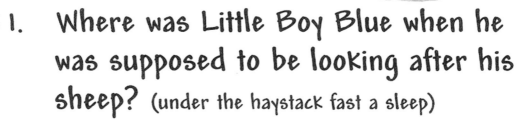

1. Where was Little Boy Blue when he was supposed to be looking after his sheep? (under the haystack fast a sleep)

2. Can you finish this rhyme? "Little Bo Peep has lost her sheep and can't tell where to find them. Leave them alone and they'll come home. (wagging their tails behind them)

This really proved to be a great time for all and got the parents involved, with laughter and time to mingle with each other after the play and to enjoy refreshments.

# Mother Goose Party Treats & Recipes

## 3 Blind Mice Treats

2 attached soda cracker squares
3 black seedless olives
1 piece yellow cheese
Layer the above ingredients on
to the 2 attached soda cracker squares.
Add one Chinese noodle in each
Black olive for the tail. Cover the
olives with cheese. Then put in a warm
oven to melt the cheese – just
enough to make the cheese look like a
blanket..

# Mother Goose Recipes
## (continued)

## <u>Pease Porridge Hot or Cold</u>

Hot or Cold Apple Cider
or

Nine Days Old

(Add one scoop of vanilla ice cream to each
cup of
hot cider to make the ice cream melt and
look like it is old porridge!)
After the plays, Mother Goose
had candy treats for the students from her
"Many Pockets Apron."

## ...A fun time was had by all...

# Mother Goose

## Some drawings of our play's characters

46

# Bookmarks

## Given to the students during our Mother Goose Unit

### Made with Rubber Stamps on card stock

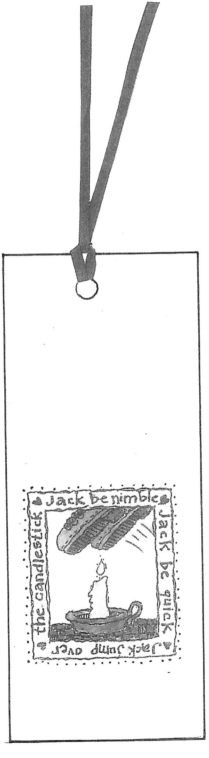

Never underestimate the power and learning skills of your students.

# Somebunny Special

Send a note home with the date and time (two weeks ahead) when the student is going to be "Somebunny Special." The child is to bring one grocery bag full of their favorite toys, books, trophies, etc. to school on that date.

Parents are invited to come to their child's presentation when his or her photos, toys, and favorite things are shown and shared with their classmates. The student tells the class about the items that they brought. It was usually done at the end of the afternoon on Mondays.

Have a table on which to display their items and remind the students that it is just to look at and not to be touched. Their items are on display for the rest of that week and sent home on Friday. The presentation should last no more than fifteen minutes. The classmates listening may ask questions after or during the presentation, whatever works best.

Before the end of the presentation, the children say why they think the "Somebunny Special" student is special. They say things like, "He's friendly," "She invited me to her house," "She is helpful," "He's a good soccer player," etc. Give students suggestions before the first student is "Somebunny Special" to give them ideas on what they might say. It is not mandatory for everyone to say something. You record what the students say about the Somebunny Special student and send the comments home to the scrapbook-keeper mother. Remind the Somebunny Special student to remember to say thank you to classmates at the end of the presentation. Give the students suggestions early on as what they might say to thank their classmates.  If they have a big brother or sister at the school, they may be invited also, as it is then special for the whole family.

The presentations were given once a week. I did it first, bringing my special things, so the students would get the idea on what they were supposed to do.  It is fun, and the parents loved it.  It is also good PR. One other thing I did was take a photo of the students with their displays and have it included in their scrapbooks.

I LOVE READING IN MY SCRAPBOOK WHAT MY CLASSMATES SAID ABOUT ME!

# "I'm Somebunny Special" Bulletin Board

Attach the written page "What my classmates say about me" here on the bulletin board and also put a copy of it into the student's Scrapbook.

## Student's name written here

Table display of student's items to be placed under the " Somebunny Special Bulletin Board."

# I'm Somebunny Special

## What my classmates say about me!

(Write classmates' comments made to the "Somebunny Special Student" after the presentation and add this page to the "Somebunny Special Bulletin Board display.")

# Blue Ribbon Helper

(Introduce this activity in November)

When a student has done seven helpful things at home without being asked, they receive a Blue Ribbon Helper Badge. Parents record the tasks their child has accomplished on the Blue Ribbon Badge Form that I send home. The student then returns the completed form to the teacher.

Prior to passing out the Blue Ribbon Helper form, we talk about helpful acts and what that might include. When their charts are completed, they come to the front of the classroom with their charts and share about their helpful tasks with their classmates.

Then, the class cheers for the student. The student's name is written on the Blue Ribbon Helper Poster and he or she receives a Blue Ribbon Badge. (Sample badge is in the upper right-hand corner of this page and was made out of construction paper.)

# Blue Ribbon Helper

*I REALLY WANT TO BE A BLUE RIBBON HELPER!*

Student's Name_____

Today I helped

1._____

2._____

3._____

4._____

5._____

6._____

7._____

Write down seven different helpful things that your child has done without being ask and record them. Return this to school by the end of November.

Parent's Signature_____

# Blue Ribbon Helper Chart

# Stuffed Animal Day

Looking for a fun way to get my students started writing stories, we decided that they should write a story about one of their favorite stuffed animals. Most wanted to bring their teddy bears, and others wanted to bring their favorite stuffed animal to school. So we ended up calling it Stuffed Animal Day.

They were to bring their animals in a bag and put them in their cubbies until we had our Stuffed Animal Party. My students enjoyed bringing and sharing their favorite stuffed animal to school to share with their classmates. What fun we had that day as each student shared their animal in front of their classmates and read the story that they had written about it. It was a fun way to introduce creative writing. Animal crackers were served after the readings!

# Marco Polo

## Classroom Traveling Bear

BEAR DAY

Nothing compares to a good reliable teddy bear!

Meet Marco Polo, the traveling teddy bear for our classroom. Whenever a student in our class (or the teacher) would take a trip, they always took Marco Polo along. Then, the student and his or her parents or the teacher would write a story titled, "The Adventures of Marco Polo." The stories were put into our Marco Polo Scrapbook.

As you can see in the photo on the next page, Marco Polo has a new sweater that he got when he traveled with one of the students in England.

I HOPE MY FAMILY CAN TAKE MARCO POLO ON A TRIP SOMEDAY...

Whenever Marco Polo had a new adventure with someone, they always took photos of his adventures. Then the student and parents would write a story to put in our class booklet. What fun it was for the students and their families to have Marco Polo as a traveling companion.

We also had a map posted in our classroom so we could keep track of his travel adventures. It was a fun learning experience for all of us.

Marco Polo

# Butterfly Unit

Photo fun of students during our
"Butterfly Unit." Taken in our classroom,
the students loved holding the butterflies and
watching them fly around in the room!

# Adopt a Senior Citizen

One of the most rewarding things that you can do for your students and yourself is to adopt a local senior citizen for your class.

My students drew pictures for our senior citizen at first and eventually wrote notes later in the school year. They loved doing this, and it is an excellent opportunity to talk about helping make a senior, who may be very lonely, smile and feel comforted in his or her senior years. The man our class adopted was at a nearby retirement home. The students made cards and drawings for him throughout the school year. They were sent through the district mail. We also had a field trip to his retirement home, surprising and celebrating his birthday with him. This was truly rewarding for the students and me, as well as their mothers and our senior citizen. It was a fun and rewarding experience for all involved!

FUN!
FUN!
FUN!

Having
lunch and fun with our
"Adopted Senior Citizen!"
He always had a BIG SMILE
when he saw us!

# Birthday Celebration

## for our Senior Citizen

Our senior citizen had been a member of our original school board when our city formed its own school district in Sedona, Arizona. This Kindergarten class of mine and their mothers continued celebrating with this senior citizen every year until his death six years later, at the age of ninety-eight. His request upon his death was for a Celebration of Life Party. He requested that these faithful students speak at his party.

Three of the students spoke, along with our superintendent, other adults in the community, and myself. What a wonderful party with family and friends to celebrate his life. Our adopted senior was an inspiration to all of us. It was such an opportunity for the students and me to be a part of his life.

This photo above is of the kindergarten students at a birthday celebration with him at his retirement home.

# Our Senior Citizen's Birthday Celebration

This photo was taken at the retirement home with some of the kindergarteners in attendance to help celebrate.

# Celebrating our Senior Citizen's Birthday!

(At his Retirement Home...Ages 96 and 97!

# Celebrating our adopted senior citizen's ninety-eighth birthday

At school, every student that read with our senior citizen through the years came to greet him on his birthday along with their teachers.

Pictured below is a parent volunteer dad who was very active in our classroom. He loved being involved with his children, both of whom I had in kindergarten. He acted in one of our kindergarten patriotic programs that was presented to the entire student body.

Below is a photo of a dad helping our class celebrate our adopted senior citizen's ninety-ninth birthday! The entire student body at our school came through the "birthday line" to thank our senior citizen and to wish him a happy birthday. Not only did he volunteer many years at our school but he was also on the first school board when our city finally had its own school district. Each student he had ever helped read through the years gave him a birthday greeting. Until his death, he volunteered at school listening to younger pupils practice their reading skills.

# Senior Citizen's Ninety-eighth Birthday Celebration

...with the cute kindergarten moms!
(his favorite photograph!)

# What fun we had through the years with our Senior Citizen on his birthday

K-Kids
and moms
first year
with our
Senior Citizen
and
again years
later
with grown
K-Kids
and
K-Teacher
Mrs. Nelson

# Class Photo Album

During the school year I took photos of various things that went on in the classroom. These photos were put in our classroom's photo album.

Twice during the school year, the photo album was sent home with each student for their family to enjoy. The students were to bring the photo album back within the next two days so another student could take it home. I kept a record of who had taken the photo album home so each student would at least have two or three times to take it during the school year, depending on the number of students in the class. This is a great way to keep parents, especially those who work and cannot volunteer, visually involved in what is going on in their children's classroom. The parents really enjoyed and appreciated this photo album being sent home.

I'LL BE GLAD WHEN IT IS MY TURN TO TAKE HOME THE CLASS PHOTO ALBUM!

# Classroom Photo Album

Please enjoy this album of photos taken of activities and artwork in our classroom as well as other special classes at school. Please return it within two days. Thank you.

# Welcome to
# Mrs. Nelson's Classroom
## "Great Fun and Teaching Series"

## Hop on the Bus
## Climb Aboard the Train
## Jump in the Wagon
## Soaring in a Hot Air Balloon
### ...as the "K-1-2 Journey" begins!

A great teaching series of four books
full of unique ideas and fun
for teachers and their eager students!

Author – Patty Nelson, Sedona, Arizona
Illustration – Carolyn Smith, Colorado

Printed in the United States
By Bookmasters